Father Callistus Cayetano
In His Own Words

"The word of the Lord came to me, saying: Before I formed you in the womb, I knew you. Before you were born, I dedicated you. A prophet to the nations, I appointed you."   ---*Jeremiah* 1: 4

I, the Lord of sea and sky,
I have heard my people cry.
All who dwell in deepest sin, my hand will save.
I, who made the stars of night,
I will make their darkness bright.
Who will bear my light to them?
Whom shall I send?
Here I am, Lord. Is it I, Lord?
I have heard you calling in the night.
I will go, Lord, if you lead me.
I will hold your people in my heart.
                    --- *"Here I am, Lord" Hymn by Daniel I. Schutte, 1981*

Dedication

To my mother who was a humble, hard-working housewife. She suffered from a nervous breakdown for years and gradually got over it shortly after I was ordained a priest. What a joyful moment in my life when they carried me to the altar for my ordination on August 15th, 1973, at Holy Redeemer Cathedral.

To my father as a Catholic teacher, who spent at least 25 years in the classroom. He was more than a teacher because he was a farmer and a farm demonstrator.

To my parents, my siblings, my friends, the parishioners, and the many other people who have prayed for me and encouraged me to be faithful, I dedicate this writing in loving gratitude to acknowledge God's call and my response as his priest for 49 years.

Father Callistus Cayetano In His Own Words

Reverend Father Callistus Cayetano

Judy Lumb, Editor

Producciones de la Hamaca 2022

Published by *Producciones de la Hamaca*, Caye Caulker, Belize
<producciones-hamaca.com>

ISBN: 978-976-8273-32-1

Father Callistus Cayetano In His Own Words

This book was printed on-demand by Lightning Source, Inc (LSI). The on-demand printing system is environmentally friendly because books are printed as needed, instead of in large numbers that might end up in someone's basement or a dump site. In addition, LSI is committed to using materials obtained by sustainable forestry practices. LSI is certified by Sustainable Forestry Initiative (SFI® Certificate Number: PwC-SFICOC-345 SFI-00980). The Sustainable Forestry Initiative is an independent, internationally recognized non-profit organization responsible for the SFI certification standard, the world's largest single forest certification standard. The SFI program is based on the premise that responsible environmental behavior and sound business decisions can co-exist to the benefit of communities, customers and the environment, today and for future generations <sfiprogram.org>.

Producciones de la Hamaca is dedicated to:

—Celebration and documentation of Earth
    and all her inhabitants,
—Restoration and conservation of Earth's
    natural resources,
—Creative expression of the sacredness of
    Earth and Spirit.

Contents

Foreword

He never holds back on a healthy laugh. His laugh is fulfilling, genuine, and joy-filled. This laugh is Reverend Father Callistus Cayetano's way of showing much appreciation and gratitude to his friends for their continued care and the companionship they have maintained.

I met Reverend Father Callistus Cayetano when I started to discern my life as a priest of God in late 1970. He was my spiritual guide for over a year. Then, in 1981, I left to study for the priesthood.

In seeing this priest, I see first his humanness, a human on a mission. He is always about that 'more' that needs to get done. He is about providing for the spiritual needs of his people, this church entrusted to his care. He serves without being complacent. He could spend hours in the confessional, as long as his people's needs are being fulfilled.

His big stature can easily be interpreted as one to be feared, as one who is a control freak. He, instead, is about dialogue with his people. He is about meeting and listening to others. He encourages others to take the lead in planning and serving their church. Overall, his patience is very noticeable in his manner of love and service to God's people.

This patient servant is poor, living truly the spirit of the gospel. With the little he has, he remains a truly happy person; with the little things he possesses he would still try to share that with others. This patient servant, Reverend Father Callistus Cayetano, is truly a man for others and not for self.

To God be the Glory!

Most Reverend Lawrence Sydney Nicasio
Belize City, Belize
March 10, 2022

My Family

My Father

My father was Frances Benedict Cayetano. He was born in Barranco on the 9th of March 1915. His father's name was Pascasio Cayetano who was married to Apolinaria Mejia. A little after my father reached the age of two, my grandmother was returning to Barranco from Punta Gorda along with her compadre, in a dory with my father in half of a pataki, a basket that was made to be waterproof.

He was secured with blankets in the basket. She was using a pole instead of a paddle. She stood on the stern to push the dory along. After they had passed Mother Bush Point, a wave hit the dory and it overturned. My grandmother fell out and my father's basket was carried to the shore where there were mangroves. He remained there.

Some men from Barranco were observing the dory, and recognized that there was a problem, so they paddled there. They didn't find my grandmother or her compadre, but they heard my father crying in the mangrove. They took my father to Barranco and gave him to my aunt Hilaria Mejia, the mother of Dr. Joseph Palacio. Hilaria took care of my father for about three or four years. By this time my grandfather, Pascacio, had found another woman, Eustaquia Shatuyei, so he married her and had her look after the children, including my father.

My father grew up with his stepmother and everything went on well until one day when my father was a pupil teacher in Barranco, she asked him to do a humiliating chore, to empty the chamber pot that had stool and urine in it. By this time my father was already dressed, prepared to go to school as the pupil teacher. So, he said, "No, I won't do that. I am ready to go to school."

She answered, "If you don't do that, I won't wash your clothes or cook for you."

My father left the house, weeping. Frederick Nicholas came by and heard my father weeping, and said, "let's go home." Frederick was living with his grandfather, Sotero Nicholas, who was my father's uncle. Frederick told Sotero that my father had just walked out of the house. Frederick asked if my father could stay with them. Sotero said, "I see how you have suffered, so you can stay with me."

Sotero had three sisters, one of whom was the side of Inocente Zuniga (Mafia). She chatted with her sisters, discussing my father's situation, that Sotero was getting old and he couldn't deal with my father. They asked Sotero if they couldn't raise him up because Sotero was too old.

Sotero said, "Yes, but I have to speak to your husbands."

Mafia said it was OK, so my father ended up living at Mafia's house. My father got married out of Mafia's house. He continued teaching. My father married my mother the first of January 1938 in Punta Gorda.

My Mother

My mother was born on the 23rd of February 1923, so next year will be her 100th birthday. My mother's mother, my grandmother, Benita Nuñez, was living with John Nepalmson Lucas. They had two other children, Augustina and Robert Lucas. My grandfather was a promising businessman in Punta Gorda. While he was doing his trading, hauling bananas and pigs from the Sarstoon to Punta Gorda and on to Belize City, my grandmother was managing the shop and the home in Punta Gorda. My grandmother suggested inviting her niece to help out running the shop and he agreed, only to find out that it was the beginning of the end because my grandfather had an affair with her niece, Clautilda and her family threatened to take him to court if he did not marry her. He sent my grandmother to her mother,

Genevieve Nunez, my great-grandmother, who lived in the Nehi section of Punta Gorda.

It happened that my grandmother was pregnant with my mother when my grandfather sent her to her mother, so it was in Nehi that my mother was born. Fortunately, my grandfather did not disown my mother. Even though my mother was not living under his roof, he still provided for her needs. So, my mother was raised by her grandmother.

My grandmother Benita came to Barranco to visit relatives. In Barranco a cabinet maker, Catarino Ariola, fell in love with my grandmother. Catarino Ariola was a jack of all trades. Along with being a cabinetmaker, he played the guitar; he was a barber; he was a good farmer; and a fairly good leader, so he was elected to be Alcalde in Barranco Village. My grandmother then moved to Barranco to live with him.

My grandmother Benita fell in love with the farm, called Trial Farm, and dedicated her full time to the farm. She grew cassava, plantain, bananas, gooseberry, pineapple, and sugarcane. She loved fruits. She also raised chickens, ducks, turkeys, pigs, and took care of the cattle. To keep up with her work, she woke up very early to make and serve breakfast, and then spend the rest of the day in the farm, returning home between three and four in the afternoon to make supper. Catarino Ariola and Benita Nunez had two daughters, Antonia and Virgilia Ariola, so they were half-sisters of my mother.

My mother was attending school in Punta Gorda. She was big for her age, so my great-grandmother, Genevieve, was afraid that my mother would fall in love with a suitor in town, so she took her to Barranco to live with my grandmother, Benita Nunez, who had married Catarino Ariola. While she was in Barranco, Frances Benedict Cayetano fell in love with my mother. They were married in Punta Gorda on the first of January 1938. My mother's father, John Nepalmson Lucas, had a big boat so he brought all the people to Barranco for the wedding celebration.

Both of my parents had suffered in their earlier years. My father lost his mother, but he was discovered in a basket after she had drowned. My mother's father, John Nepalmson Lucas, sent my grandmother to Nehi, Punta Gorda, when she was pregnant with my mother. But God blessed both of my parents with life, health and 14 children, five girls and nine boys.

My Siblings

My mother gave birth to Bernard on the 20th of August 1940 in Barranco. My father kept on teaching and was transferred to the beautiful village of San Antonio Rio Hondo in Orange Walk. He spent some years there. The 21st of November 1942 I was born there in San Antonio. My father was the principal and teacher in charge of San Antonio Roman Catholic School at the time. Also living there with my father and mother were my uncles Silas and Moses, and my aunt Virgilia. They all helped to nurse me in San Antonio up to the age of four years. Silas and Moses are the sons of my grandfather's second wife, after my grandmother drowned.

My brother Nathaniel called "Shorty" was born 29th of May 1945 in Orange Walk Town. My father was transferred from San Antonio to Monkey River and taught there, where my twin brothers, Fabian and Sebastian, were born on 13th January 1947. From Monkey River my father was transferred to teach among the Q'eq'chi Maya of Dolores in 1950. In 1951 he opened the school in Otoxha.

Joseph was born in Punta Gorda on the 21st January 1949; Alfonso on 29th of October 1950; Fatima on 30th of January 1952; and Ignacia on the 3rd of January 1954. There were two sisters who died when they were two or three years old, Jane and Genevieve. Jane went with my mother on a trip to Punta Gorda and the boat capsized. She drank too much seawater and couldn't be revived. Genevieve died with my father in Otoxha. She caught some sickness, possibly pneumonia. They were isolated out there, and my father didn't have the medicine for her. It was a sudden thing. She was buried in Otoxha. Then came Robert who was born in Barranco, and John who was born in Crique Sarco. Claudia, who was born in Punta Gorda, is the youngest of all.

My Childhood

Dolores and Otoxha

I was fascinated with church. Even when I was very young, I admired the different priests when they came to celebrate Mass in Dolores and Otoxha. I said "I want to be like that. I want to be a priest."

Fr. Andlauer, S.J., came to Dolores and Otoxha periodically. He gathered the children together and tested their knowledge of the faith and how well they knew the prayers in Q'eq'chi. If they did well, he gave them prizes, like a rosary or a holy card. It was a way to get them to pray in their own language. I don't hold this against him, but I was one of the few Garifuna who joined the Q'eq'chi children. When it came to me he gave me the longest prayer, the Confession of Faith, and I was to say it in Q'eq'chi. I don't remember if I said it OK and got a prize. I was in Infant II when the Education Officer came to visit the school in Dolores. I must have been five years old. Mr. Brown was his name. He questioned me a number of times and I answered all of his questions. That is the first time I remember doing well in school, impressing the Education Officer.

Traveling from Barranco to Otoxha was a long journey, so my father woke us up at two in the morning to start. We went first from Barranco paddling to the Temash River for one half hour. Then we paddled up the Temash River about 12 hours to Crique Sarco, getting there by three in the afternoon. My father was the only adult, and we were all children, but he didn't mind. He did it for the sake of the family, to keep it together. Throughout most of the journey we sang hymns and songs along the way. I looked forward to that trip. We were guided by the stars, in the morning it was the morning star going up the river to Crique Sarco. Coming back in the evening it was the evening star.

From Crique Sacro to Dolores we walked 12 miles, or if we were going to Otoxha we walked nine miles. At one point we had to cross a falls in the Temash River. When the river was low, we just held hands with our brothers and waded across.

But sometimes, especially during the rainy season, like in July, the river was flooded. There was a time I witnessed my father almost losing his life crossing the river in a strong flood, called "top gallon," meaning the river had swollen very high. Owen Louis, the officer who had come from England to work with the Q'eq'chi, had put up a ferry for transport at this crossing. It was the first time we were using this ferry. We thought the cable was connected to the ferry on both ends, but it wasn't connected. When my father finally got the ferry to move, he thought we were strong enough to stand on the ferry and pull on the cable to get the ferry across. A pulley should have been there, and the connection made, but nothing was there. The flood was high, and it began pulling the ferry downstream. It was stronger than we were. There were some men from Otoxha who had come along to carry our things. They were the first ones to get tired and give up. That weakened the whole thing. Then we also put down our hands, and my father was the only one still holding the cable. The current was pulling the ferry and my father fell into the current with his long boots on. I thought that was the end of him. Thank God he came up just in time to grab hold of the ferry.

From there we went to Monkey River and then he was transferred back to Dolores. In Dolores a strange thing happened, a mischievous act. I saw boys flying kites. I was tempted to fly a kite, too, but then for some reason we dipped our kites into kerosene and set them on fire. My kite landed on the roof of the school, so the school burned down. My brother Bernard and I were held responsible for burning the school down. It was my first time going to prison, a part of the cabildo, community center, the Alcalde's courthouse. We would go home for supper and spend the night at home. In the morning after breakfast, they took us to the cabildo. That went on for two or three days.

When people in Otoxha heard that the school had burned in Dolores, they decided to build a school in Otoxha and invite my father to come to teach there. So we moved to Otoxha. The people in Otoxha helped to bring our things there about six miles northwest. Some parents in Dolores who loved education sent their children to Otoxha to school. They would walk the six miles.

In Otoxha my mother fell ill in the early 1950s. My father had gone to Punta Gorda to sit the teacher's exam and my mother stayed alone with us, the children. She suffered a nervous breakdown. The Alcalde sent word to my grandmother in Barranco to come to look after my mother, so my grandmother organized people from Barranco to go to Otoxha, paddling from Barranco to the mouth of the Temash, and then up the river to Crique Sarco. Then they walked nine miles to Otoxha.

The people from Barranco did that at night and got to Otoxha about one AM. They carried a Coleman lamp to light the way on the road.

Paul Palacio was a good friend of my mother, so when she heard his voice, she recognized him and calmed down. She had forbidden us to take any food from people in Otoxha, but I think we still got our tortillas. Antonia Palacio and Virgilia Lorenzo came and took care of my mother. We walked back to Crique Sarco, then passed through the hands of the alcalde and then we were free to continue to Barranco. Because of having a sick person, you had to get the permission of the alcalde. My mother was seriously ill, but he granted permission, so we went back to Barranco in their big dory called the Recuero. She had to be restrained because they were afraid she would jump out of the boat.

Barranco

Even when I accompanied my father to the stations where he taught, I spent school vacations in Barranco Village. The holidays were a great time for my siblings and cousins, grandchildren of my grandmother, Benita Ariola. We went to the farm to plant rice. We were all young people going as a group and we were rowdy and mischievous. We were supposed to put in 5 – 7 seeds in a hole, but we would put in 15 – 20 to hasten the process. When harvest time came, she saw what we had done and told us about it later.

My grandmother prepared nice lunches of boil-up. Even though there were many of us, she was able to feed us all. We had coconut water, cashew, gooseberry, craboo, pineapple, oranges, and sugar cane. My favorite was breaking the cohune kernel to get the nut. My brother Joseph got the brunt of that. He was holding the nut. The head of the axe hit his finger. One of his fingers is shorter or spread out because of that. During the day we went to the farm and in the evening we had our own entertainment as a family in the home. Some of the boys sang songs, recited poetry, and we prayed together at the end of the evening. I always looked forward to that.

In 1953 and 1954 I was living in Barranco to look after my mother, so I went to Primary School in Barranco. I remember in Standard 4 we had a good teacher, Vilma Chimilio. She taught us very well. I fell in love with her teaching arithmetic. Candace Arzu gave a test to Standard 4, 5, and 6, and I got the highest grade. Those who did well on the test were promoted from Standard 4 to 5.

I was in Standard 6, just promoted in 1954. I used to play football a lot. I played lots of positions, right wing, left wing, and many times I was selected to be the goal-keeper. When I was eleven years old, I dislocated my right knee, so I was laid up for a while. My grandmother Benita Ariola nursed me, but her way of nursing was painful. She asked a question, "After you get better will you go back to playing?" While asking, she was pulling out the leg and it was painful. Because of the pain I was more concerned about the end of the treatment than the answer to her question. Three weeks later I was back on the field in Barranco. She reminded me of the injury, but I just brushed it off. But it did take me twelve weeks to completely recover.

Punta Gorda

Early in 1955 my father and mother agreed that I would go to Punta Gorda to live with my grandfather John Nepalmson Lucas. I was to take care of household chores, cooking the food, sweeping the house for him. He insisted that I go to Mass every morning. Saturday mornings he would take me to the plantation and on

Sundays, he would send me to church. January through April 1955 I was in Standard Six at Peter Clavier Primary School in Punta Gorda. Sister Therese, a Pallotine Sister, was my teacher. It was from her that I sat the Primary School Leaving Examination in 1955 and I passed.

In Punta Gorda my grandfather was a candy maker. The name of this candy was "Hug Me Tight." I had to sell it on the streets of Punta Gorda. I was mischievous and I joined my friends to play marbles instead. One day it was getting late, and I was in a hurry to sell some candy before I got back home. In the midst of rushing, the jar of candy fell on the ground and broke. I wanted to disappear. I didn't want to go back home at all because I knew a big lashing was waiting for me. It was the first time my grandfather showed me mercy, saying "I won't lash you this time, I will save it for next time."

I was fascinated with church in Punta Gorda. Even though he didn't go, my grandfather sent me to Mass every morning, weekdays and Sundays. I thank my grandfather for this initiative because it was the beginning of the promotion of my vocation to the priesthood.

On Saturdays he took me to the farm a mile and a half behind Punta Gorda. He had ground food: sweet potatoes, yams, and yampi. We went early to harvest the ground food, so by late morning or early afternoon we were walking back. For some reason there were many of us on that same road going to different farms and coming back at the same time. I often ran up to a school classmate, talking as we were coming back.

When we got back home, both of us were hungry. I was the cook. I peeled the sweet potato, ripe plantain, yams, and cassava, and prepared a nice boil-up. I put some fish on top and boiled it. The kitchen was a simple open one with four posts and a roof. It had a fire hearth that used firewood. It was not far from the beach, so the sea breeze would blow through and through. But the breeze wasn't blowing this particular day, so I had to fan the fire with a hat. Maybe I was weak or half asleep, as I was fanning the fire, I don't know, but the hat touched the firewood and that moved the two stands the pot was on, so the pot fell down. My grandfather heard a noise and asked what is happening. I said, "the pot fell, but I will take care of it." Since it was open and near the beach around noon, the people who were looking for fish, waiting for the fishermen, could see our kitchen. My aunt Ku heard the commotion and saw what had happened. Ku loved to tease, and she was only too happy because now she had some material. She had witnessed the whole thing and heard my grandfather's remark. She always reminded me of that incident when I visited her house.

Back to Barranco

After I passed my primary school in Punta Gorda, my grandfather was talking of moving to the farm during the week and coming to town only on weekends. I couldn't see myself walking all the way from the farm every day to school, because the house in town was near the school. I had already passed my primary, so I left my grandfather and went back to Barranco. Passing the primary meant that you could be a monitor who supervised a class in a primary school.

When I got to Barranco, I went to my grandmother Benita Ariola's farm. She said, "why aren't you in school?" So I went back to school. The teacher was Candido Arzu, who asked me to help with Standard V. I was to correct their work. After a while I was monitoring Standards V and VI. I did that for almost two years. For the last four months I was getting a stipend of $5 a month, $20 for four months. Pupil teachers were drawing a salary of $17 a month. After primary I was to join

Candido's son, Nolbert, preparing for a scholarship. We were both the same age, but I failed the scholarship exam. Nolbert did well, got the scholarship, and went to high school. I kept teaching in Barranco and taking classes for the pupil teacher exam. I taught in Barranco from 1955 until May of 1957.

Moving on from Barranco to Belize City

In April 1957, Fr. Marvin O'Connor, General Manager of Catholic schools, offered my father a scholarship for one of his children to attend St. John's College (SJC) because he was a good teacher. My brother Bernard was going to Lynam Ag College in Dangriga, so I got the scholarship. In July of 1957 I traveled on the Heron H to Belize City to attend St. John's College.

It was from a schoolboy from Barranco to a young man in Belize City. The daily activities and the night life were both quite different in Belize City. I did a lot of walking to high school in the morning and coming back in the afternoon. The night activities were spending hours studying between 6 and 9 PM during the week. Then on Saturday nights I enjoyed the sea breeze on the shore.

I attended SJC, an all-boy's high school at Landivar, from 1957 through 1961 while boarding at Teacher's Hostel on New Road. Across New Road was a house where young girls from Central America that were going to Saint Catherine's Academy were living. The boys from Central America that were going to St. Johns were living on campus. In the evening after supper and on weekends we would sit in the veranda looking at each other across the street.

As a student of SJC, I got involved in sports, mostly football. I also joined the Boy Scouts at Holy Redeemer and got involved with Sodality, a religious society for young people going through adolescence. I was 15 years old when I joined. It was to deepen your spiritual life, encourage you to say the rosary every day, which was a commitment one made to become a member of Sodality.

Attending SJC was like a continuation of what my grandfather had begun earlier. Here I attended Mass daily, Monday to Friday, then Saturday and Sunday at Holy Redeemer Cathedral. We had Mass at 11 every morning and at 11:30 they dismissed us for lunch. Alan Burns was my friend in the same class. His mother was Nessie Burnes and his father Andrew Burns owned Angeles Press. Alan would bring lunch that his mother had made, and he shared it with me. That gave me the strength to play football while I was waiting for my lunch. It would leave me 10 minutes to have my lunch.

In my four years in Belize City living at the Teachers' Hostel I developed a liking for people from other parts of the country. We had students from all over the country, some on government scholarships, others on Catholic mission scholarships.

I joined the Boy Scouts in 1958. In May of 1958 we went to San Pedro to camp for three weeks. I really enjoyed that. I was playing a lot of football as goalkeeper. I played on the Junior team at SJC, and the Senior team. But that wasn't enough for me, I joined the City team in the evening, Saturday and Sunday. I played for both my Junior and Senior years, always as goalkeeper.

At night I loved listening to music on the radio. On New Road was a bar and dance hall and we could hear the musicians practicing there. I fell in love with dancing. On holidays I went dancing both in Punta Gorda and Barranco. In Belize City SJC's Senior Class had a prom to celebrate graduation. I knew Gungi from Dangriga because my father had taken in her mother, Sylvia, before I was born. She shared her experience with my father with her children, so her children were anxious to meet us and help us in any way. I was close to Gungi who encouraged me to do well in school and offered to take care of my needs. Whatever I needed, she would provide the money to purchase it. That gave me confidence, motivated me to apply myself to my studies and do well in school. I promised her I would take her to the prom. I never did go through with that because I did not return to SJC in July of 1961. Instead I went to teach in Crique Sarco. That year Hurricane Hattie hit Belize City, so there was no prom.

I must also pay tribute to Fr. Leo Doyle for his influence and inspiration nurturing my vocation. In 1960 I was in Third Form in high school. That was his first year as an older priest assigned to Punta Gorda. He had been an army chaplain. He was very active and enthusiastic. When he learned that I was going to SJC and interested in becoming a priest, he coached me. I only went up to Fourth Form and then I applied to be a teacher. I didn't need the Fifth Form to be a teacher.

Teaching

Crique Sarco

When I graduated from SJC in 1961, I asked to be posted to Crique Sarco as my first teaching appointment as an Assistant Teacher to Teacher John Zuniga. Fr. Weber had sent me to teach in Barranco, however, I thought that Barranco already had too many SJC graduates teaching there. Many wanted to be in Barranco, but just a few would go to an isolated place like Crique Sarco. I had already spent a year and a half helping out in Barranco, so I thought it was time to go somewhere else. I didn't return to Belize City for graduation, which was in December because I had already started teaching in Crique Sarco, so I was spared the experience of Belize City in the aftermath of Hurricane Hattie.

I spent six months in Crique Sarco. The next year Rev. John Paul Cull, S.J., transferred me to Otoxha where I taught in the school that my father had opened eleven years earlier. I stayed there for two years and six months. I was impressed with Fr. Cull's determination and missionary zeal trekking through the rainforest to cover these missions. He usually spent two days in Otoxha, hearing confessions and celebrating the Eucharist, baptizing, performing marriages, and preparing children for confirmation.

As a young teacher I was touched by his religious zeal. I wanted to do more than just teach. I thought by becoming a priest, I would be able to take care of spiritual and educational needs of the people. I asked Fr. Cull to investigate the possibility of my becoming a Jesuit priest. He looked into it, but because my grades were not that impressive, they would accept me only to be a Jesuit Brother. I said, "no, no, I don't want to be a Jesuit Brother. I want to be a priest." I thank God for this, because belonging to a religious order like the Jesuits would not have been consistent with the way I envisioned life as a priest.

Otoxha

Then I went to Otoxha in 1962 where I was the principal. Fabian was teaching there, too. He was there ahead of me a whole year with Elias Palacio as Principal. In April of 1964 I attended a retreat in Belize City. I spoke to the retreat master about my calling to the priesthood and he said he would talk to Bishop Hodapp. The Bishop said he would accept me, but he would send me to Corozal to see how the Diocesan priests were living. In Otoxha there would only be Mass every two weeks when the priest came. The Bishop wanted me to experience Mass every day.

Corozal

By July 1964 Bishop Hodapp had arranged for my transfer to Corozal where I would be teaching at St. Francis Xavier Primary School and living downstairs of the Rectory where the Diocesan priests were living. I was supposed to see how they were living as priests and see if I would like that kind of life. What I liked about it was how the priests were living together as locals, not as a cloistered religious order. The Sisters looked after me. I was alone with the Fathers; Martin Avila was the Pastor. I was sent to be with him. He took me under his wing.

I didn't realize that there is minor seminary and major seminary. Even though I was teaching in the primary school, that experience in Corozal was also an abbreviated minor seminary from August 1964 to January 1965.

But there was a big problem. My father and mother got sick. My father had retired from work as a Farm Demonstrator and he had fallen ill, so he was not earning the usual money. We experienced extreme poverty, especially my mother. I shared that with Father Leo Doyle in Punta Gorda. He said to continue my studies, that he would help my family. My father accepted it, but my mother didn't accept it.

Seminaries

Seminary in Honduras

With the coaching of Fr Doyle and Bishop Hodapp, I entered seminary on the third of February 1965 in Tegucigalpa, Seminario Major de Nuestra Señora de Suyapa in Tegucigalpa, Honduras. I joined five seminarians, Santiago Boyton, Joe Castillo, Elias Pech, Lloyd Lopez, and Kurt Kasebeer. During the first four years of Philosophy, you have philosophy, natural sciences, mathematics, and the arts. Then Theology started the second four years. Around my time they were changing it. They were cutting down the Philosophy to three years with four years of Theology. Theology incorporated psychology, sociology, church history, cannon law, music, the sacraments, scripture, and liturgy. The school year went from the beginning of February to the end of November, which was divided into two semesters, February to June, and August to November. I finished a year and a half in Tegucigalpa.

My spiritual life got a boost at the Seminary with the help of the Canadian priests who ran the Seminary. They are known as the White Fathers from Canada. They taught in Spanish. They were learning the language, just as I was getting to learn the language, so we were in the same boat. The spirituality that I got there was the traditional spirituality heavy influenced by the divine office, Lauds were morning prayers and Vespers were evening prayers. Those would be the prayers that the Monks in their congregation prayed every day. As diocesan priests we were limited to the two hours of lauds and morning prayer. Along with this we had the celebration of the Eucharist. We had the Mass in the morning after we prayed the morning prayer. After Mass we would go to the Rec Room for breakfast. In the evening at the end of the day's work, around 5:30 we would have evening prayer. After evening prayer, we went to the place where we had our meals.

Our classrooms in the Seminary were close to the chapel. We had classes from 8 in the morning to 11:30. After that we went to lunch and then had a rest period from 12:30 to 3:00. It was during that time that we also played soccer, practice games among ourselves. In sports, we had two things. We had recreation football (soccer) and ping pong, table tennis. The enrollment at the Seminary was 26 seminarians. Six of us were from Belize.

One thing that impressed me was the Thursday night Holy Hour, but it was all night. The Seminarians took turns, one hour each. When your turn finished, you could call the other one to take their turn. We would have at least two Seminarians praying, connecting with Jesus. That really impressed me, that holy hour at night.

We had a carpenter from Tegucigalpa who came in and taught us how to make armed chairs. That was the carpentry that we learned at the Seminary.

The Second Vatican Council ended on the 8th of December, 1965, at the Feast of the Immaculate Conception. It left a lasting impression on us because the church was in a state of change. From the traditional we were opening more to the world. That was my first year at the Seminary. Our Rector, the priest who was in charge of the Seminary, shared the content of the Bishops' meetings at Vatican Council II, so we were able to follow the content, so much so that when I left the Seminary in Tegucigalpa, there was a continuity with the Seminary in the United States.

Two documents from Vatican II were *Lumen Gentium, the Light of the World,* and *Gaudium et Spes, the Church in the Modern World.* We as Seminarians learned about the change from the old, traditional way to a more open liberating point of view. The church was opening herself to the world. That was really important. The church was changing for its own good.

In Missouri, many of the Benedictine monks had gone abroad to study and come back to teach there. They were putting into practice what Vatican II had just said. I felt the call being very close to Vatican II. I was really involved with the changes in the church.

Seminary in the United States

Then in August of 1966 Bishop Hodapp sent the four of us who were continuing our studies to the United States, two candidates to Kenrick Seminary and Santiago Boyton and I went to Immaculate Conception Seminary in Notaway County, near Maryville, Missouri, which was run by the Benedictine fathers. At Conception Seminary I finished my studies in Philosophy. They gave me one year of credit for the year and half of study in Tegucigalpa, so I started with their second-year students. And I did two years of Theology there.

While there I was adopted by Maud and Antonio Sandoval, an American couple. Tony is Mexican-American, a Catholic through and through. He was teaching Chemistry at the University of Missouri at Kansas City. Maude was African-American, a convert from Methodism to Catholicism. The way I met them was through the Seminarians from Kansas City. In 1966 every Saturday evening, Seminarians would drive to Kansas City and I would ride with them. The Society of our Lady of the Most Holy Trinity (SOLTS) had a center where they would go over the readings for Sunday. Father McChugh introduced me to Maud and Anntonio at this meeting. Maybe they came into being at the time of Vatican II. They wanted Mary to be their patroness. That was a new religious congregation, Seminarians trained to become priests.

The summer vacation of 1967 I was in Kansas City. The Holy Name Parish invited people from the suburbs to experience the inner city. Together we did home visits in the city for the Parish. A Dominican was in charge of the Parish. Before we went out, we went over the readings we would use in the homes. It was very effective. We used the scriptures as a jumping board to discuss what was happening in the neighborhood. We got to know each other, the city and suburbs. My accent helped because those in the suburbs knew I was not from the city and so did those in the inner city. There was a lot of respect that came from listening to each other.

I was playing soccer at Conception Seminary. A few days before the 4th of April 1968 we were playing against another school. I tore the cartilage in my right knee and was taken to the hospital in St. Joseph, Missouri. I was in the hospital during the funeral of Dr. Martin Luther King, so I watched the whole thing. I was really impressed with the preachers and the singing. I really thanked God that I got a chance to watch it. It helped me appreciate the man because of the tributes they were giving. I spent six weeks recovering.

That was a big moment for me because it was the same year I spent summer holidays in Toledo, Ohio, where I joined a Diocesan group of young people who worked among the Blacks in the inner city. My group was examining housing to see how we could improve the situation. There were two big things that happened to me in Toledo, Ohio. Fr. Bernard was the priest in charge of program and we got along well. He took a group to Washington for the Poor Peoples' March. We spent three days there in the crowd. We also marched on the buildings, Senate, Congress, singing the Civil Rights songs.

One or two weeks before the Poor Peoples camp ended, we heard about Los Santos, the team from Brazil with Pele that was going to play in Cleveland. So we organized a group, got a car and a driver. We left about 1 pm and got there before the game started. At the end of the game, a friend and I jumped the fence to go and greet Pele. I told her, you give him an American kiss and I will just embrace him. Then we went back to look for our ride. We got back to Toledo the next morning, tired, but we were able to go through the day.

The summer of 1969 I went to New Orleans. I fell in love with the jazz. Almost every weekend I was in the French Quarter listening to jazz. We were working with the poor in the Desire area of town. One of the beautiful things was organizing an item of entertainment from the Desire area, dancing, singing, and poetry. Groups who ran summer programs all over New Orleans entered in this large event and we came in second. The young people were very happy about that.

The summer of 1970 I went to an Indian reservation in New Mexico. I joined Bishop Jerome Hastrich in Gallop, New Mexico. Navajos and Pueblos were there. I looked forward to the powwows. I really enjoyed that. It was the first time I was able to admire their skill and knowledge. The way they had been painted to me was that they were poor and incompetent, but it was not like that at all. They were very artistic making clothes for sale, almost like the Maya in Toledo.

One of the important things we did together in the Seminary was to wake up early in the morning to do our exercise. We would trot down the road, where the train was coming from. Even during the snow, we got up and did our walk. I encouraged him to join me and play soccer and volleyball. Two of us from Belize were Black Seminarians. We were given a special task to be public relations (PR), especially for Bishops who were visiting the Seminary. We would go and serve them. As PR we also had a special task, when we had big feasts, like the feast of the Immaculate Conception, we would help serve the food to the Seminarians. After the Seminarians got through eating, we would eat and drink as much wine as we wanted, the leftovers from the celebration.

I spent hours praying in the Chapel at the Seminary, or I joined the Benedictine monks for the morning prayer (Lauda), and vespers, the evening prayer. Seminarians were not required to attend. It was voluntary. We had Mass in the evening, which was required, and after that we had supper. Since I was a slow eater, I was among the last to leave the Refectory. Along with the Chapel, the other place I really enjoyed was the library. I spent hours going through books, doing my homework in the library. I had a Spiritual Director at the Seminary whom I visited at least once a month for counselling and guidance.

Disenchantment with the U.S.

In fact, the whole experience in the U.S. was full of shocks like that. I had the impression from my readings in school in Belize, Catholic basic readers, that the best people in the world live in America and America was like heaven. So I wanted to go there. The priests who came from there to Belize were kind and nice. At Conception Seminary we seminarians were introduced to the pastoral program Saturday afternoon when we went into the city to take a census of the high-rise buildings and see the filth and everything. I found that very hard to understand, so all that about America came crashing down. This was in the context of 1968. I thought this is not the place I envisioned from Belize.

That experience also took me into Mexico along the border, Guymas. I spent three to four weeks there and suffered a culture shock. The way the Mexicans reached out to me was like coming home to Barranco, quite different than going to the Seminary. There was a distance in the Seminary. The closeness in Mexico was emotional for me. I was able to identify with those people. When I got back to the Seminary, I missed that closeness. I became disenchanted with the climate at the Seminary. I felt emotionally drained. Cynicism and sarcasm were what I was getting from the other students. I wanted to get out of there. I questioned myself, what kind of priest I would be. I thought those that finished in the U.S. were too Americanized, that they had consumed too much of the American society. I was thinking that in two years' time I will be ordained as a priest and I want to go back to Belize, but I don't want to go back to Belize as an American.

So, I wrote Bishop Robert Hodapp to look for another seminary for me outside of the U.S., in Jamaica or any country in Africa. The summer of 1971 I got a job through Fr. George Clements with the Archdiocese of Chicago in a summer resort conference center for eight weeks. I was assisting a young man who had a lot more experience running the place. I shared with Fr. Clements that I had written my Bishop requesting a change in Seminary. June and July had passed, and I hadn't heard anything. Fr. Clements said, "I just read in the paper that your bishop was shot in the Miami airport. He wasn't killed, but he is recovering."

Seminary in Mexico

I had made up my mind that I was not going back to Conception, so I thought I had better try two places in Mexico, one in Guadalajara where there were 500 students. The other was Seminario Consiliar de Mexico in Tlalpan. I thought Guadalajara was a bit conservative and Mexico City was better. I had saved up US$500 and I was able to travel all the way to Mexico City, then to Belize with only $100 using trains and buses. When I got to Mexico City, I checked with the Seminary to see if there were openings and what I had to do. There were openings and I had to ask the Cardinal for permission. Thank God I was able to save $400. Bishop Hodapp had recovered and was able to take care of my case. He said he would talk to the Cardinal. He called and was able to get right through to the Cardinal, who recognized Bishop Hodapp's voice, remembered him. Bishop Hodapp said he wanted to ask a favor, that he had a seminarian who wants to get into your Seminary and the Cardinal agreed right then and there.

But in 1971 the church and the seminary were not recognized by the government because in the revolution they separated from the church and that continued for some time. Only after John Paul II they eased that some. So, theoretically, I wasn't supposed to be there. I went into Mexico as a tourist, which gave me 90 days, enough for one semester. I was able to pay tuition for that whole year with US$100. After that, to get a student visa, I had to be enrolled in a government-approved school. The Jesuits had their own school, but it was a bit expensive. I heard that the University of Mexico only charged 2,000 pesos for foreigners. I was able to pay my whole year with US$100. I took classes at the University of Mexico, classes for people who were preparing to work in the foreign ministry, such as anthropology. In the morning I attended Seminary at Tlalpan (8-12:30) and then in the evening (4-8) I studied at the University. I got help. It is a good thing about the Mexicans. When they like you they will help you. I was able to do well in the classes in both institutions.

One other thing helped me. In 1972 the students went on a strike and shut down the university, so I could concentrate on Seminary. I was running out of my US$, so that helped, too, as I wasn't required to pay their fees, but I still kept my student visa. I paid for my third year of theology and then I wrote Bishop Hodapp saying, "I have done my part and paid for my third year. Now you will have to pay for the rest," so he agreed.

It was in Mexico City that I was ordained a Deacon. There used to be Sub-Deacon, Deacon, then priest. I was ordained a Sub-Deacon in 1971, and Deacon in June 1972 in Mexico City. You serve as a Deacon for a year, and at the end of year you are ordained a priest. In August of 1973 I was ready to be ordained as a priest. Some of those from the Benedictine Monastery came to Belize for my ordination.

Mexico City was the saving of my vocation and the deepening of my love for our local church, the common person. My concern was that our own people own the church. This is what came through to me very strongly from the Mexican Seminarians. I saw that, whereas in Belize people no longer liked to go to church, so churches are empty most of the year, in Mexico and Guatemala the churches are filled. That situation in Belize concerned me.

Ordination

On the 15th August, 1973, Bishop Robert L. Hodapp ordained me as a priest for the Diocese of Belize. Before I was ordained my brothers Sebastian, Fabian, Joseph, and Alfonso thought that it was time to build a better house because the one my father had built was falling down. So they decided to do it and have it ready for my ordination. It was a gift for me. We had a nice reception after my ordination at the house in August of 1973.

Cayo

I was first assigned to Sacred Heart Parish, San Ignacio, working with Fr. Oswald Reyes as Associate Pastor. I was sent to replace Fr. O. P. Martin who was transferred to Belize City. At Sacred Heart Parish I visited the missions in the villages on Sundays to conduct Mass. I visited with the teachers, the children and the parents in the homes to see how things were going. I was continuing the work of Fr. Martin.

While there, the American couple that had adopted me in Missouri, Maud and Anthony Sandoval, came

---

The poem on the next two pages by Marcella Lewis in English and Garifuna is from her book, *Walagante Marcella: Marcella Our Legacy*, 1994. Producciones de la Hamaca, Caye Caulker, Belize.

Walk with Truth

Walk with Truth.
Truth will lead you on the right way
You might stumble on your way
Do not be afraid
Call on the Master
He will stretch out his hands to you.
For He is with you

Walk with Truth.
Truth will lead you in the right way

It will rain on you
The sun will burn you
Do not complain
You will enter into darkness
Call on the Mother of our Savior
The brightest star will appear
She will lead you to Light

Walk with Truth.
Truth will lead you in the right way.

There will be days when you cry
Your patience gone
Call on the Almighty
He will help you; you will arrive with gladness
If you believe in our Master

Walk with Truth.
Truth will lead you in the right way.

In the name of the Father,
In the name of the Son,
In the name of the Holy Spirit, Amen

Béibuga Luma Inarüni

Béibuga Luma Inarüni
Ladundeirubadibu inarüni lidoun üma le richabei
Bachugeraguba luagu béibuga
Máhüchüraba
Waba luagu Wabureme
Lichugubei lúhobu bun
Ladüga anirein buma

Bubaronguoun, béibuga luma inarüni
Ladundeirubadibu inarüni lidoun üma le richabei

Láhuyubadibu huya
Sü lábume weyu
Makeraba
Babeluruba lidoun luburiga
Waba luagu Lúguchu Wabureme
Táfuaruba waruguma to durungua timá boun
Tadundeirubadibu lidoun Larugounga

Bubaronguoun, béibuga luma inarüni
Ladundeirubadibu inarüni lidoun üma le richabei

Ñéibei weyu bayahuagu bówagua
Gumuha bugurasu
Waba luagu Súntigabáfu
Liderubadibu, bachülürüba lau aban ugundani
Anhein afien bubéi lidan Wabureme

Bubaronguoun, beibuga luma inarüni
Ladundeirubadibu inarüni lidoun üma le richabei

Lidan liri Úguchili,
Lidan liri Irahü,
Lidan liri Áfurugu Gúnfuliti, Ítara la

to Belize and recruited me to join them in introducing the Marriage Encounter Movement in Belize. Father Jim Gallagher of Marriage Encounter arranged for me to buy a new Land Rover for this work. From 1974 – 1976, I was heavily involved promoting the Marriage Encounter Movement countrywide. I am very grateful for that opportunity of working with so many couples and families in Belize. Thank God Bishop Hodapp was supportive and encouraged me to continue my work in Marriage Encounter. I traveled the entire country to promote Marriage Encounter without ignoring my mission stations in San Ignacio.

Two Tragedies

On the 12th of June 1976 my father inexplicably set our brand-new house in Barranco on fire. My brother Nathaniel had the custom of leaving containers of gasoline in the house. This evening when my father returned home at night, he lit a match and threw it on the ground, not thinking anything. But he must have thrown the match on gasoline and that lit up the whole thing. My mother, John, and Claudia were in the bedrooms and jumped out of windows. My father was trying to get out the front door, but he was already on fire. He was taken to Punta Gorda and from there flown into Belize City. I met him at the airstrip and took him to the hospital. He was serious so he stayed in the hospital. My Uncle Silas was living in Belize City, so he looked after my father. I came from San Ignacio to visit him in the hospital.

Then on the 6th of July, 1976, while returning home from my mission station of San Luis at 9 p.m. alone, hungry and half sleepy, my brand new Land Rover overturned with me. This was like Saul's experience with the bright light. Saul was knocked off his horse and I fell from the driver's seat to the passenger side in my Land Rover. After awhile I turned off the engine, turned off the lights, and managed to get out the passenger side by the roadside. I spent an hour and a half calling out to God for help. About 11:30 p.m. I saw two vehicles with their bright lights on and I said, "Thank God, help has come." So that bright light that Saul saw, I saw it, too. My own conversion was from being half-hearted to fully giving myself to the missionary work.

People returning to their tourist resort had two vehicles. One took all the passengers to Blancaneau Lodge. The other turned around and took me to the hospital in San Ignacio. I had a broken pelvic bone. I spent three days in the hospital in San Ignacio then went home to Sacred Heart Rectory. Fr. Oswald Reyes looked at me and said I should go to Belize City to be under Bishop Hodapp's care. He took me to Belize City Public Hospital to get better treatment. From there Uncle Silas appeared on the scene to further assist in my recovery. He had a friend who was good at massaging and got him to massage me two or three times a week. That was really helpful and hastened my recovery. I spent three months recovering at the Catholic Presbytery at Holy Redeemer Cathedral in Belize City. By the middle of September, I was walking again slowly. The 8th of October 1976 my brother John went with me to Toledo in the same Land Rover that had been repaired.

San Luis Rey, San Antonio, Toledo

Before the accident, Bishop Hodapp had recruited me in March of 1976 to serve in Toledo among the Maya Mopan and Maya Qeqchi with Father Mesmer. It seems that Bishop Hodapp was impressed with the missionary work I was doing in the missions in Cayo and Marriage Encounter, so he thought I might transfer that same zeal to working with the Maya in Toledo.

I accepted, but when I shared the news with my brother priests, they were against it, saying, "They are sending you there to die." That was the negative view by the local priests of coming to Toledo to work with the Maya. They knew I would have to walk a lot. Then Bishop Hodapp said that the Jesuits in San Antonio would support by paying for me to fly from Punta Gorda to Belize City for meetings. They would offer me facilities, too. I didn't have to worry too much. After my accident everything quieted down. Because of my condition, I wasn't attending meetings, so there was no more discussion. Around October 7th or 8th, I was ready to take on the journey to San Antonio, Toledo, to join Father Mesmer to work among the Maya. He accepted me and wanted me to be co-pastor with him at San Luis Rey in San Antonio. That worked out well.

After I went to San Antonio to take up my duties, all the opposition I had heard calmed down. Nobody brought it up. I was the one who had my own fears that I had to overcome. I overcame it by faith in God, by prayers. Also, my brothers John, Robert and Nathaniel helped me. Working with Marriage Encounter I had developed confidence and a strong missionary zeal to serve the church in Belize. I was able to go all out for Marriage Encounter. After my accident as I was going to San Luis Rey, I thought I was losing the zeal and would have to start all over again to build up the zeal to work with the Maya. Even though I had accepted, I had my own fears, first because of my accident and also because it was the first time a local priest would be working with the Maya. Before that only the Jesuit priests had been working with them.

My vehicle was fixed and I was able to drive it from Belize City to San Antonio. My brother John was willing to accompany me on that trip. I joined Fr. Messmer who was already working at the San Luis Rey Parish in San Antonio, Toledo. I was afraid that I would not be able to manage the rigorous life because there were hills that we had to climb, and I was still recovering.

The First Village Tour

For the first trip to the villages, Father Mesmer took John and me to Punta Gorda. My brother Shorty was waiting for me at the pier in Punta Gorda to take me in his dory up the Sarstoon River to San Pedro Landing, six miles from Dolores. We got to San Pedro Landing at 1 o'clock in the morning. We slept at the landing and waited for the dawn to walk to Dolores. We left our bags at San Pedro Landing. That helped me a lot. I didn't have to carry anything, just walked.

Gradually as I walked, I felt more comfortable walking. Then another worry came along. I worried how the people in Dolores would accept me because I had grown up as a little boy in Dolores. Would they accept me returning as a priest?

We got to Dolores just before the people went to the plantations, so they heard the bell and came to church. The Alcalde and the Mayordomo for the church supported me. Their word was listened to and obeyed. Two men from Dolores went back to San Pedro Landing to get my things. I spent the night and then went to Otoxha and back to Crique Sarco. From there Shorty came to take me back to Barranco and Punta Gorda.

Village Tours

The usual tour to visit villages started in Aguacate. Father Mesmer and I took turns going to the villages in the deep south. One time I would drive him to Aguacate and he would go on the walk. The next time he would drive me, so the people had priestly visits every two months. After Father Mesmer drove me to Aguacate, I spent the night and the following morning two carriers helped me walk to San Benito Poite where I spent two nights there and went on to Otoxha. Both of those roads were very hilly, so I spent two nights in each, then two nights in Dolores, two nights in Crique Sacro, then one night each in Corozan Creek, San Lucas, Mabil Ha, Santa Teresa, and then Aguacate where Father Mesmer would pick me up.

Each time I moved, two majordomos (young men) were assigned to walk with me to the next village, carrying my things. The more I was walking, the better I felt. The fear of falling down left me. God held me by the hand. The good thing was that my brother John came to go on these walks to the villages, so there was no reason for me to panic. John was in the Belize Defense Force and able to take time off to accompany me on these journeys for two years, until 1978.

My assignment was working fulltime with the local Catechists in the surrounding villages. There were twenty-nine villages in the San Luis Parish, 19 of which were reached by driving, and ten were reached only by walking, including, San Antonio, Santa Cruz, Santa Elena, Pueblo Viejo, Jalacte, San Vicente, San Jose, Crique Jute, Mafredi, San Pedro Columbia, San Miguel, Silver Creek, Big Falls, Indian Creek, Moody Hill, San Isidro (Dump), Holy Trinity (now closed), San Felipe, and Santa Anna.

Most of these villages on the road are people that came from the deep south and speak Qeq'chi. People in San Miguel came from Santa Teresa; Big Falls people came from Crique Sarco; and Silver Creek people are from San Miguel and San Pedro Colombia. San Antonio, Santa Cruz, Santa Elena, San Jose, Crique Jute, and Pueblo Viejo are all Maya Mopan. Blue Creek is mixed Qeqchi and Maya Mopan. Jalacte and San Vicente are Qeqchi, but they are recent migrants from Guatemala.

Those two villages are near the border. The catechists in those two villages were trained in Guatemala and seemed to be more progressive at that time.

There were two kinds of healing. The walking helped the pelvic bone to heal, and I didn't have to carry anything because I had help. That was the physical healing. The spiritual healing was overcoming the fear of being able to do that walk. The quality of liturgical celebrations, praying with the people, took on a new meaning for me as I joined them in giving thanks to Almighty God for accompanying me on the journey from village to village and ministering to the Qeq'chi people. Completing that journey allowed me to overcome the fear. I thank God for that. My involvement in service to the people in the villages, preparing my homilies, helped me to realize that I was doing the prophetic part of the journey.

Team Ministry - 1977-1981

I continued my missionary activities among the Maya people of Toledo. Fr William Messmer and I were co-pastors of San Luis Rey Church in San Antonio, Toledo. In 1977 Sr. Rose and Sr. Marion Joseph joined Sr. Caritas Lawrence working in San Luis Rey Parish. They joined Brother May, Fr. Messmer and me to form the Parish Team Ministry. All six of us in the Team Ministry were given team-building training by a priest from the U.S. and Sister Lynn, a Sister of Charity who worked in Dangriga. I enjoyed working as a member of the Parish Team Ministry. They challenged me to grow, and I challenged them to grow. We had regular meetings to evaluate our work as part of the fruit of the team training.

We were coming from different cultural settings. Sr. Caritas was from Belize City; Sisters Rose and Marion Joseph, Fr Messmer, and Br. May were all from the U.S. We were in a Maya Mopan and Qeqchi setting where we were ministering to the Maya people in Toledo. I was privileged because I had grown up among the Qeqchi so it was not difficult for me to work among them. It demanded on my part to keep the team focused on the Maya Mopan and Qeqchi people and not to mix in the cultural baggage from the U.S. At the time I didn't realize what was happening, but inculturation was going on. I made a deliberate effort to remind us that we were not going to impose ourselves on their culture but get to know the culture and work within it. We evangelized in a humble, yet faithful way, respecting the culture. We were countering the effect of the Protestants who were interfering with the local culture. This is why Bishop Hodapp wanted me to come to Toledo to help stem the growth of the Evangelicals who were proselytizing and promoting looking down on their own culture and taking on the values of the Evangelicals.

We were building their self-esteem in their own culture, but also making them realize the effects of their bad habits like drinking and their way of celebrating Christmas and Easter. But also we wanted them to appreciate the beauty of their community and family life where the men would help each other fell their plantation and the women would come together to prepare the food so that at the end of work in the field they would come home to a nice dish of caldo, which was keeping the family spirit together. The first fruits of their labor were celebrated making a special offering to God for giving them a good harvest that year. They invited the community to enjoy green corn porridge from the harvest. There was a tremendous spirit of oneness in the community, caring for each other.

As a representative of the Team Ministry, I did basically the same Pastoral visits to the communities that I had done with my brother John, except some villages were added, like San Marcos along the Southern

Highway, not far from Dump. The complete circle took about two weeks. From November 1976 to April 1984, that was my routine to walk among the villages. The people in villages looked forward to these visits and planned their activities around them, like baptism of a newborn, and wedding feasts, along with first confession, first communion, and confirmation.

After a while even that walk became routine for me. The same thing caught me with Marriage Encounter. I began to take it for granted. To me that accident was very important to remind me not to take things for granted. Part of it is taking God for granted, instead of letting God lead me, I think, "I have to get this done." The accident was a wake-up call for me. We all need wake-up calls to get out of the ruts we fall into.

We worked with the people to build their churches. The villagers were supposed provide 75 percent of the labor and materials for the church building, and 50 percent for the school building. The Catholic Mission would provide the rest. It was good see how the Maya Mopan and Maya Qeq'chi Catholics responded to this new program. It had a social element to it. Each village would also support the elderly of the village by helping to make a plantation for them, fell the trees, burn, and plant. They planted corn, rice, and beans. One year's worth of corn was given to the elderly. Beans and rice were sold in Punta Gorda to raise funds for church or school projects.

Each village had either a church building, or a place to celebrate Mass, and most of the villages had a school building run by the Catholic school management. After Father Messmer left I took over the schools, too. The same way I met with the Catechists in the villages, I met with the teachers in all the schools every month as a group. Every month when they were in school with the help of the secretary, we made out the pay sheet and sent it to the government. They would approve it and send the sheets back with the money. We made out the checks and distributed them to the teachers. I tried to have a good working relationship with all the teachers in the area. I thought this was the best way to show support and encourage them to give their best. I visited the schools often.

We all looked forward to the Christmas vacation because on the last day of school, the teachers came to San Antonio, and I spent a day with them. In the morning we had in-service training. Then each school was expected to produce an item for entertainment. There was socializing among ourselves and that helped to create a good spirit. My dream was to eventually have the catechists in the church training the parents who would train their children at home. The teachers would train the children for their first communion and confirmation in the school. I wanted both groups, teachers and catechists, to be on the same page with religious instruction. So the catechists would do their part in church and the teachers in the school. That was partially met, not in all the communities, but in quite a few of them. That was good to see them working together for the building of the church.

One of the highlights in the villages was taking part in Holy Week services, especially Palm Sunday when people from different villages would walk and meet in one village. We would have Mass and then a short meeting with the catechists and prepare ourselves to walk with Jesus on the Stations of the Cross on Friday, and on Easter Sunday to celebrate the Triduum, the three days from Holy Thursday to Easter Sunday. It was an important part of my work to prepare the people. In 1980 we invited Bishop Hodapp , S. J., to come on Palm Sunday to San Pedro Colombia. He enjoyed that visit. He even rode a horse and played the part of Jesus. He had been invited to go to El Salvador for Bishop Oscar Romero's funeral, but he decided to come to San Pedro Colombia instead.

I am very grateful for God's blessings on this ministry among our people. It has proven to be a very fruitful ministry. I was convinced that the answer to our people keeping their faith was for them to have ownership of their church. An example is how we got the Catechetical program translated into Q'eq'chi. Fr. Messmer and I spent Christmas and Easter together in 1976 and 1977, but our experiences of Christmas and Easter were far from being Christian. At the end of the Christmas feast, Fr. Messmer would have to take people who were chopped up to the hospital in Punta Gorda. The same thing happened at Easter. What kind of celebration was that? It turned Fr. Messmer's vehicle into an ambulance as a result of violence against each other, including wife-beating. Neither the Christmas nor the Easter messages were getting through. There was too much drinking. There was no new life.

We heard about good programmes in Guatemala for indigenous people in Coban and San Pedro Carcha. They had workshops training the people to be good church leaders, using their own language to read the Bible and sing and pray in Q'eq'chi, to worship in Q'eq'chi. Fr. Messmer went to Coban and learned a little bit of Q'eq'chi. Then I went for six weeks to brush up on my Q'eq'chi and learn what the church was doing with these people in Coban, Alta Vera Paz, Guatemala.

What helped was Radio Tesulotlan. The people could tune in and hear their own language spoken. They had good programmes for empowerment. We decided to do our own thing in San Antonio, so we invited some of the men who had started the Cursillo programme to give our first weekend retreat in San Antonio, Toledo.

We invited 100 people, Mopan and Q'eq'chi. Mostly men came, but they were really touched by the Spirit. This was genuine evangelization. This was exactly what I wanted to be involved in, evangelization before sacramentalization. But in Belize we were doing it the other way around, sacramentalization and then lip service to evangelization.

The main workshop was in San Antonio and afterward we made visits to the villages to see how the leaders in each village were doing. You could see the hunger in the people for this kind of thing. They were really taking it in; they were responding. We still had the Christmas and Easter celebrations, but without liquor, so the violence was greatly reduced. Then it completely stopped. This was the answer to my prayers. The beauty of this was the building up of the community, the solidarity, helping out each other, and witnessing the flourishing of the faith, like a new Pentecost.

I enjoyed the Holy Week services, especially Palm Sunday and Easter Sunday when large gatherings from the different villages were coming together to celebrate their faith in God. Palm Sunday was always a big deal in Toledo. Each year the big gathering was in one particular village. This year, 2021, the big gathering was in Dolores. By now we have done at least one gathering in all the villages.

We were doing wonders in the sense that the Q'eq'chis were using their own resources to collect funds to put up their own church buildings. The people came up with some unusual fund-raising. They would fell a plantation, plant beans and rice, and then use the proceeds for the building fund.

One of the villages that took the lead in this was San Benito Poite. They bought the zinc, had the lumber (mahogany) cut nearby, and Fr. Mesmer and I supplied the cement for the floor. For transportation of the cement and some of the sand, we secured the services of the British Forces, so we got it in by helicopter. Fr. Messmer and I were close to the British soldiers who had a camp at Salamonca Crique Jute about four miles from San Antonio. We transported the materials to Aquacate and the helicopter took it on to San Benito Poite.

One year Santa Rosa and some of the villages on the road near Dangriga were hit by a hurricane. The people in the San Luis Rey Parish made a collection all the way from San Pueblo Viejo to San Pedro Columbia. They brought food to San Antonio and had an all-night vigil. Then two truckloads traveled to Dangriga to distribute food to the victims of the hurricane.

Around that same time there were a lot of activities in the church. Each Parish in the Diocese promoted something. In late 1978 we had our first church assembly meeting. Catholics from all over the country came to Belize City. As a result of the petition, we made in that first assembly to have one of our own locals as the next Bishop, Bishop Hodapp, along with the Papal Anuncio, ordained Osmond Peter Martin as Auxiliary Bishop of Belize on October 7, 1982, just a year after Belize's Independence on September 21, 1981.

Fr. Messmer was there until 1981 and then I was there by myself. I was supposed to get help from my brother Alfonso, who had been ordained in June 1980. After his ordination Alfonso was assigned to La Immaculada Church in Orange Walk and then he was assigned to Punta Gorda to work with Fr. Howard Oliver. But Fr. Oliver died, so then my brother Alfonso was by himself in Punta Gorda. He was supposed to help me, but before he came there were two priests in Punta Gorda, so with Fr. Oliver's death and Fr. Mesmer's departure, we were short two. He had fewer villages and he was young and healthy, so the Bishop thought since we were brothers it would work, but we two were trying to do the work of four priests.

Pope John Paul II

I was always charmed by Pope John Paul II. He was the first Pope whose elevation to Pope struck me from the very beginning and I was able to follow him up to the end. After he was elected Pope in 1978, the Latin American Conference of Bishops was preparing for a continental meeting of Bishops in Puebla, Mexico, to be inaugurated by the Pope in 1979. I was so taken up with it that I was determined to go and attend the Latin American Conference of Bishops. I got myself in as an interpreter of Spanish to English for the Bishop from the Caribbean Antillean Diocese.

The Pope made his visit coincide with the Conversion of Saint Paul, the 25th of January, 1979, which was celebrated at his first stop in the Dominican Republic. He went on to Mexico for the meeting of the Latin American Bishops. I flew from Mexico City to Oaxaca to witness the Pope's visit there where he was warmly welcomed. I was struck by the Pope's address to indigenous people at Oaxaca where he made a call for respect of indigenous people.

When they announced that Pope John Paul II was coming to Belize in 1983, we brought a delegation from Toledo to welcome him. On the 9th of March 1983, John Paul II celebrated Mass at the Belize airport. As he was receiving, our Holy Father lifted up a little Q'eq'chi boy in his arms for all to see. It was Marcos and Manuela Makin's son, who was about four months old. I was privileged to shake hands with Pope John Paul II. By that time the faith had picked up and the Q'eq'chi people were living their faith.

Our Lady of Guadalupe

I visited the Basilica several times while I was still a seminarian in Mexico City from 1972 to 1973. I prayed and put my work in the hands of Our Lady of Guadalupe. Towards the end of my work in San Antonio, San Luis Rey Parish, I took six catechists along with me on a pilgrimage to the Basilica of Guadalupe in Mexico City in July of 1983. As a group from Belize, we offered our missionary work to the care of Our Lady. We thanked her for the positive response of the indigenous here in Belize, especially the Maya Qeq'chi and Maya Mopan.

Like Adam and Eve, the eyes of four of my leading catechists were opened to the materialism they saw around them on this pilgrimage. They were touched by it so much that they asked for a raise in their salary when we returned from the pilgrimage. I was alone then. Fr Messmer had gone on to Corozal. I was running the whole program myself. These were coordinators, special catechists. They did very well until the experience in Mexico City when they saw all kinds of things that they wanted to buy. But they needed money for that. They worked for money, so they charged more for their service.

That really challenged me with the Qeq'chi and Maya Mopan leaders in the church. When they asked for raises, I told them I could not afford that. So, they said that they would find other ways to earn a living and moved to greener pastures of other churches. Some coordinators were bought over by the foreign missionaries and played a leadership role in the Evangelical and Pentecostal churches. Fortunately, not all of them went. Towards the end of John, Chapter 6, when Jesus was talking about the bread of life, Jesus told the crowd, unless you eat my flesh and drink my blood, you will have no life in you. Many of them in the crowd left. Then Jesus turned to his disciples, asking, "will you leave, too?" Then Peter answered, "to whom will we go?" Those coordinators who stayed had that same kind of response.

Medellin, Columbia

From the 24th of April to the 9th of December 1984, I took a sabbatical and attended a wonderful refresher course in theology in Medellin, Columbia, "Pastoral Teaching in the Church". But I came home to a difficult situation. My brother Alfonso left the priesthood at the end of 1984. The letters I got from Belize didn't tell me anything about what was happening. I arrived on the 8th of December and was to meet with Alfonso in Punta Gorda a few days later, but that never happened because he had already packed up his things and left. Then I was assigned to both Parishes. Bishop Martin had just been elevated from Auxiliary Bishop to the Bishop fully in charge of the Diocese of Belize. This was a shocking situation for him to manage. To hold over in December and January, I was assigned to Punta Gorda to run both Parishes. I had priests coming to help out on weekends, but during the week I would take care of both parishes. I spent time in San Antonio and Punta Gorda and the people who wanted to see me would come into town. There was a lot of uneasiness at that time because the Protestants were around converting people.

Orange Walk

La Immaculada Parish in Orange Walk

Bishop Martin then assigned me to work in La Immaculada Parish in Orange Walk from February 1985 to August 1991. I was born in San Antonio, Orange Walk, so it was a joy for me to return and minister to my own countrymen, *paisaños*. But I understood when Jesus said that no prophet is accepted in his own country. I would have thought I would do better than the other priests, but I was just the same as the others.

One of the highlights of my assignment to Orange Walk was the honoring of Our Lady, La Immaculada, by large crowds of Catholics from all over the country during the Marian year on the Feast of the Assumption on the 15 August 1988. I didn't realize until later that was also my 15th anniversary as a priest.

In Orange Walk the drug trade was heavy. I had been following the drug trade even from Toledo because our small church building in Moody Hill, close to Golden Stream, was a pick-up point. There used to be a quarry where they would pick up stones, but it was abandoned, so the men used that to store their stuff and the trucks would go there to pick it up. The drug barons were familiar with the people and told them that whatever they grew they would buy. We were stuck with that because it brought in quick cash. During 1982, 21 – 23 children had died due to dehydration in Toledo. The people growing rice and beans didn't have the money to take their family to see the doctor, or even if they got to town, they didn't have the money to buy the medicine. They got promissory notes instead of cash for rice and beans because the government was broke.

Drugs were the thing to do in Orange Walk because marijuana brought in more money than the sugar cane. There were kidnappings. They kidnapped Eloy Escalante, a big UDP, but the BDF got to him before they executed him. Thank God, the men involved in this knew my vehicle and were very respectful. They wouldn't let anything happen to me.

In Orange Walk we had the help of the Madrecitas de la Luz from Merida, Mexico, who ran three-week missions, two weeks in smaller villages. They always began and ended with a Mass and that was a renewal of faith. Both the priests and the Madrecitas were visiting the villages. The Madrecitas did house to house visitations and invited them for services and instructed them on their faith. That is the reason the Catholic faith in Orange Walk has taken the lead throughout the Diocese of Belize. The Madrecitas also worked with the Dirigentes, lay ministers. Each village in Orange Walk took the pride of having their own altar boys. Sometimes you would see six, up to twelve altar boys serving Mass. The families were responsible to buy the cassocks for their boys.

On Saturday evening, January 19th, 1990, when I returned from celebrating a Mass at San Estevan, Fr. Curt informed me of the death of my mother. I found it very difficult to believe at first because earlier in the day I had called to check and was told that she was improving. So, I wasn't expecting that sad news. I had made up my mind that I would continue with my schedule for that Sunday. I was to go to San Felipe, 30 miles away. Getting to San Felipe was no problem, but when I smelled the incense, I broke down. I cried all the way through the Mass. Even though I didn't want to believe it, here it was. I knew it was true. That should have been a lesson, but I continued to San Roman. On the way to San Roman my vehicle got stuck and I couldn't go forward or backward. I thought about my mother and experienced her closeness. I walked a little and found a vehicle to pull me out, but I was almost too late for the Mass.

We went to Punta Gorda for her funeral. I did not celebrate the Mass for my mother. I asked Bishop Martin to celebrate the Mass and Fr. Lloyd Lopez had the homily. Most of the Diocesan priests joined the Mass in Punta Gorda. After the funeral, I kept on with my schedule of the villages in Orange Walk. Regular things were the Lenten Season, preparing for the penitential life of the church in Orange Walk. The celebration of that Lent became my bereavement. I really grieved over the death of my mother. I was far from her. I was away when she died. A heavy weight came down on me. I was reminded of my mother's love for us, her children, and the need to keep the brothers and sisters together. It was her desire and my father's, too. I took it upon myself to take on the mission of grieving, but united with the rest of the family. That was the first time I felt the urgency to do something like that. That Lenten season and Holy Week meant a lot to me, celebrating Holy Thursday, the Last Supper Mass, and the Good Friday stations of the Cross of his death on the Cross, and his resurrection on Easter Sunday. That all meant a lot to me.

We had all the villages come together in one village and had the Palm Sunday celebration of the triumphal entry into Jerusalem, as well as his crucifixion on the cross. It is strange that I didn't make the connection between the death of my mother and the death of the Lord on Good Friday. I was living it in a special way. The Easter Vigil took on a very special meaning, death and resurrection of the Lord and the death and resurrection of my mother.

In the past all the children, along with my parents would come together on Easter Monday for a family gathering and renewal. I don't remember what we did on that Easter Monday, but probably following the tradition we gathered. When I was in Orange Walk, I would drive to Punta Gorda after Sunday services and stay at my brother Joe's house and bring along some goodies to share with the family. That was a practice of our family to gather both on the 26th of December, Boxing Day, and Easter Monday. After the Easter Monday celebrations, I would return to Orange Walk to continue my missionary work.

When Bishop Martin came to Orange Walk for Confirmation in 1991, he informed me of my transfer from Orange Walk to Belmopan. Just before leaving

Orange Walk, I paid a farewell visit to the churches. We celebrated a Mass of Thanksgiving for the growth of the Catholic Church in Orange Walk though my missionary work along with Father Curt Kassebeer.

Belmopan

I was assigned to Our Lady of Guadalupe Parish in Belmopan as Pastor. During my stay in Belmopan, I had to travel to Punta Gorda to bury my father who died the 29th of January 1993. Bishop Martin chartered a plane for the priests who wanted to come, and he was the chief celebrant for the Mass for my father.

When I was in Belmopan, I worked closely with the Spanish-speaking charismatic group, most of whom were refugees from El Salvador, Honduras, and Guatemala. I worked with a different group of the charismatic Catholics in Belmopan. In Belmopan, I celebrated Mass for the charismatic and heard their confessions at their codicils, three-days retreats.

When I took over the Parish in Belmopan, religious instruction was taken lightly there, like something added on, after school hours. What kind of Catholics were we producing? These are not committed Catholics. They had every right to say, "we have been to school all day and then they want us to stay after school, no!" The first thing I wanted to do was to put religion into the heart of the school day. There was some resistance at first. But the Education Officer for High School, Gilberto Chulin, said that each denomination, and especially the majority denomination, had a right to have their religion taught to them first thing in the morning. The thing was to sit down with the principal, and work out the seating arrangements, what would happen with the other students that were not Catholics. Sr. Gregoria Lizama was teaching there, and she helped me a lot.

Almost every educational Board, I was on it. For two years I was the Chairman of the Regional Education District of Cayo, which represents all the educational facilities in the District, all levels, all high schools, tertiary schools. Deacon Cathers was pushing, "why don't you ask for a Catholic School for Belmopan?" There was no opposition. At first people were saying that a high school would be easier than a primary school. But I said, "No, we will start with the primary school." Eventually we got the approval for a Catholic Primary School, so with Bishop Martin's help, we built a beautiful school with ten classrooms, Our Lady of Guadalupe Primary School. The opening of the school took place on the 11th of September 2001. I watched on television as the Twin Towers went down in New York City before I went for the school opening that day.

Dügü 1996

I must admit that I was persuaded from small not to believe in the dügü. My grandfather and my father didn't talk to me about it, but as good practicing Catholics they had to be against it. Thank God I wasn't that curious to find out what was happening. I was aware when a dügü was taking place, but as a child I didn't get close to it. But then two things happened in 1976. First our new house in Barranco burned to the ground and a month later I had the accident in my Land Rover in Cayo. While my father, my grandfather, and I did not believe in dügü, I thought there must be some connection between these two events. It was some years later before I made the connection, but then I understood that the spirits of the ancestors were crying out for attention.

When I wanted to make the commitment to the 1996 dügü that my brothers were planning, I decided to ask permission from Bishop Martin rather than going behind the door. He was somewhat positive, saying "Go, see what you can learn, what you can do." Working with the Q'eq'chi and seeing the revival of their own traditions also helped. They have a tradition of "mayehac", their way of making an offering, which they incorporated into their church life.

That 1996 dügü was the first time I actively took part in a dügü. Since it was my first experience, I was cautious and kind of leery. But I was taken aback by some of the things that happened, especially onwehani, the appearance of the ancestors. I got an understanding of how the spirits reveal themselves and bring messages to living persons. Now I understand.

One special event in the 1996 dügü was the baptism of Roy Cayetano's three sons. I had prepared Isani, Emeni, and Ibime Cayetano for baptism, but Roy didn't tell me when and where they were to be baptized. He asked if they could be baptized in the temple during the dügü. For Roy it was an act of anthropological initiation, but I took it as a sacramental thing, baptism during Mass in the temple during a dügü. The young men had been initiated into the Garifuna understanding of what it means to be a Garifuna man and initiation rights to become a member of the Catholic church, too, and that makes it complete.

Now I am completely at ease with dügüs. Buyei Estevan Palacio and I have given joint talks about the dügü from the point of both the Garifuna and the church's teachings. I don't see the church being against it. The church just didn't understand what it is all about, so through some of its members, it had taken positions that were unreasonable. It is a cultural thing. I see the healing value in my own life and among family and friends.

I have reflected a lot over the big incident the 6th of July 1976 when my brand new vehicle overturned with me. It reminds me that I was becoming selfish in my serving God and God's people, selfish in the sense that I wanted to go it alone. That was the reason for the accident itself. I had always had a driver along with me and that day I should have asked Godwin Buckley to go along with me to San Luis, a sawmill that belonged to the Wajib Habet family. Not too far from the sawmill was a government-aided Catholic school. I had gone to San Louis to celebrate Mass for the people working at the sawmill and their children. It so happened that years before, my Aunt Sylvia got bitten by a poisonous snake there. Bishop Martin, who was not yet Bishop then, took my aunt to Tea Kettle to see a snake doctor. The snake doctor did attend to my Aunt Sylvia. She went to Dangriga to recover, where she got worse and died.

My father had welcomed my Aunt Sylvia into our home. This was in the 1930s. My parents were married in 1938. So it was probably 1939 or 1940. She spent time living at home with us as a family member. Sylvia married Apolonio Lopez out of my father's house. That is important because after they left and Sylvia had children, she spoke highly of my father's kindness to her. She shared this with her daughters and her only son, Steven Lopez. Her daughters remembered those stories fondly, so much so that when I was in high school in Belize City, one of her daughters, Gungie, left Dangriga to go to Belize City to work with Dr. Goscinsky. Gungie reached out to me at the Teacher's Hostel when I was at SJC, introduced herself to me as Sylvia's daughter and that she was returning the favor to me that my father had shown to her mother. She said, "anything you want." She offered me material and financial help as I was at SJC.

Later on, my Aunt Silvia's son Stephen went to the States and sent for his sisters to come and live in the States. When I would go to visit and do special Masses in New York, the daughters of my Aunt Sylvia would invite me to their home. Angelina was one of them, as well as Gungie and Louise. They continued to share with me, continuing to return the favor that my father had shown their mother.

That trip to celebrate Mass at St. Louis, brought me back to my Aunt Sylvia's incident when she was bitten by a snake. It was my Aunt Sylvia who was present with me during my accident, 7th of July, 1976. She was protecting me from all harm and all evil. Before that she was requesting that I celebrate a Mass of Thanksgiving for her. It didn't dawn on me until now, as I write this. The dugu brought this back. She was an ahari hovering over me protecting me. When my vehicle had fallen into the ditch and I was praying, the bright lights of the vehicles reminded me of God's light coming through to help me. My Aunt Sylvia was praying for my recovery. This was a profound experience because it led me to appreciate my people's culture, the healing process, asking for forgiveness, reconciliation with the Lord. I had strayed from the Lord. I thought I could go it alone, not counting on the Lord. Even though I was doing the Lord's work, I was doing it without the Lord. This experience brought me back. God was saying to me, "what are you doing, are you playing God?" I see it as I was the Prodigal Son being brought back to the Father. It is only now that I am relating this to my accident and the burning of the family house.

This ties in nicely to that first pastoral trip when my brother Shorty was taking me to San Pedro Landing and we walked to Dolores for the Mass. My Aunt Sylvia accompanied me on that walk to Dolores, saying, "Don't be afraid. I am with you." It was as if God had sent her to be with me. It would be a good thing to celebrate a Mass of Thanksgiving for her.

The dügü comes in because my grandfather, Marcelo Cayetano, father of Pascasio Cayetano, was married to Apolinaria Maheia, who was my great-grandmother. They were requesting a Mass from my father, but then my father did not cooperate with them. So we the grandchildren decided that we would have a dügü in their honor to bring about this cultural healing, as well as reconciliation with the ahari. Because the Mass had not been done, there had to be a dugu. This was the reason for building the Marcelo Cayetano Dabuyaba Complex.

Belize City

I was assigned to Holy Redeemer Cathedral from September 2002 to September 2009. Then until August 2013 I was helping Fr. Larry Nicasio at St. Ignatius and St. John Vianney as Priest in Residence.

It is strange that Belize City was the only place I didn't want to come and work because of the violence. That really scared me. But when the Bishop said, "I would like you to come to Holy Redeemer," I said "OK." He was surprised, "No discussion?" That was good. I was ready to move on from Belmopan because we had finished the Primary School building.

The reason Bishop Martin wanted me to come to Belize City was to help Auxiliary Bishop Wright who was the Pastor of the Cathedral. He had too much work and they thought I could help him. The first two years went off well. What also helped me was that Fr. Lazarus was there. He was the Canon lawyer for the Diocese. In Belize City there is more work visiting the hospital, the sick, funerals, weddings, preparing for first confession, and confirmation.

At Holy Redeemer, I saw a promise fulfilled, that is, of working closely with Bishop Dorick Wright who was Pastor of the Cathedral and Auxiliary Bishop. When he went to the States to do his studies at the Seminary, I was already studying ahead of him at Immaculate Conception Seminary in Conception, Missouri, so I welcomed him. This Seminary is run by the Benedictine monks and priests. Here was a student from Belize who came to study for the priesthood at Conception. Even before this, Santiago Boyton and I were the first two coming from Belize to study at the Conception Seminary. Santiago Boyton discontinued his studies for the priesthood but continued living in the States. Father Dorick Wright came to take his place. As an older Seminarian, I took him around the Seminary to let him become familiar with different places, for example, the Chapel where we celebrated Mass, the Refectory where we had meals, and his room. I introduced him to the brothers and Seminarians who were there.

I had expected a similar treatment by him at Holy Redeemer. Holy Redeemer was a home for him, but I was a stranger there. I suppose he tried his best, but I expected more from him. Since I was Associate Pastor, I really threw myself into pastoral work at the Cathedral. I worked closely with the parishioners. Every Sunday evening I celebrated the Mass in Spanish. The time in Mexico prepared me well to work at the Cathedral and in Orange Walk and Belmopan. In Belmopan I had migrant workers to work with there, coming from El Salvador, Guatemala, and Honduras.

At Holy Redeemer I spent hours hearing Confessions, both of the children going to school, as well as their parents. The children came from their first communion and confirmation classes for me to hear their confessions. Their parents came before the Saturday evening Mass, so I was in the Confessional from 6 to 7 PM. I stopped just before the Mass and someone else celebrated the Mass.

At Holy Redeemer I continued hearing Confessions for the charismatic group on Thursday evenings. I also worked closely with the Spanish-speaking choir, helping them select the hymns for different seasons, going over the Sunday readings with them.

At Holy Redeemer Anthony Turton was the Sacristan, who sweeps the church, sets up the altar for the celebration of the Eucharist for Mass, and he opens and closes the church. I lent him my vehicle to drive home and then he came in my vehicle to take me to Marion Jones Stadium for exercise. We walked from the Stadium to the Fort George Hotel and back. At first, we trotted inside the Stadium, but after they closed the Stadium for repair, we decided we would walk from the Stadium to the Fort George. That was doing Anthony's free time from 1:30 to 2:30 PM. His friendship was very good for me as I was looking after my eye surgery, he was the one to drive me to the doctor and back.

At Holy Redeemer, the Diocesan priests elected me to serve as the Chairman of the group. In Belmopan I was heavily involved in the pastoral meetings and retreats at Trinidad Farm. Those involved the Diocesan priests, the religious men, the Benedictine priests who came from Cayo, and the Order of Our Lady of the Most Holy Trinity who were working out of Benque Viejo del Carmen. That was Father John McChugh's work. Then they came to Divine Mercy in Belize City. Some of the priests lived at Divine Mercy, but they served San Pedro and Maskall.

I spent seven years at Holy Redeemer. Bishop Dorick Wright decided to invite Father Noel Lesley to be the Paster at Holy Redeemer and I would work with him. I worked two years with him. Then Jordan Gongora from Yo Creek was ordained a priest, so he worked as Associate Pastor at Holy Redeemer. Since there were three of us and Holy Redeemer couldn't afford three priests, I asked Bishop Doric Wright to go Saint Ignatius to help Father Larry Nicacio who was Pastor at Saint Ignatius and also taking care of Saint John Vianney Church. Before there had been an Irish Columban Priest who built up Saint John Vianney Church, but he had gone back home. So I went to help Father Larry Nicacio. I didn't even wait for an answer from Bishop Dorick Wright to my request.

I really appreciated my time with Father Nicacio. Even though I was visually impaired, I was able to hear confessions and help out with Mass at a smaller scale. Father Nicacio and I took turns doing Mass at St. Ignatius and St. John Vianney. It was during that time that I celebrated my 40th Anniversary in 2013.

Blindness

When I was in Belmopan a Cuban doctor warned me that I was developing diabetes and I should watch my diet so I wouldn't need insulin. So, I kept up my exercise, walking around the Ring Road in Belmopan every morning, starting at 4:30 to get home at 5:30 to take a shower and drive to church for Mass in the morning. I was noticing I had difficulty seeing when I was driving. A couple of times I drove off the road, one time right into a ditch. So, I told myself this is poor judgment due to my eyesight. Dr. Hoy said take these drops and come back to see me in two or three months. Bishop Martin must have spoken with Dr. Hoy and came up with the idea that I needed surgery for glaucoma costing $12,000. A Specialist came from Guatemala and they did my surgery for glaucoma. I had lost 90 percent in the right eye. It was the left eye they were trying to save. The surgery was in 2004, but they found it was a bigger problem than they thought. The surgery was too much for my eyes. Friday I went for the right eye and Saturday I went for the left eye. Bishop Dorick Wright expected me to continue to work. I thought the surgery helped, but I was pushing myself too much getting back to work. Instead of giving myself eight weeks of recovery, I barely gave myself four weeks. I had some heavy schedules at Holy Redeemer 5:30 am Mass, even though there were only 20 people, it included George Price and his sister, influential people. That has its own challenges struggling with darkness. I would also do the 8:30 am Sunday children's Mass and the Saturday 5:30 evening Mass in Spanish. I had Fr. Lazarus Augustus helping me with the Mass.

Later on when I switched from Dr. Hoy to Dr. Valdez, he said there was a big mistake in the surgery. It wasn't done properly. When I was celebrating one Saturday Mass, I met an eye doctor from Columbia. She said, "come to Dr. Hoy's Clinic, and I can examine you." The following day I went to Dr. Hoy's Clinic, but Dr. Hoy said, "This is my patient and I don't think there is anything more you can do for him." She didn't have any suggestion. Instead of improving, I started losing more and more of the vision.

When I had the eye surgery in 2004, Father Lazarus helped me out at Holy Redeemer. After that he went to Guatemala City for medical treatment and died there. His body was brought to Belize for his funeral and burial in Dangriga.

I see bright light and I am aware of darkness and glare. Early in the morning I take a shower and put in my eye drops. When I don't apply the eyedrops, my vision is duller. Swimming helps and drinking coconut water helps. I hardly see, but my hearing is accurate, so I know who is near me. Sometimes I see people as a shadow.

With the eye drops I use now in 2022, they help me, not to see clearly to read, but more or less I can judge where I am going. In a sense the left eye hasn't gone completely. I insist that somebody lead me when I am going into a crowd. I used to have a walking stick, but it got lost when I moved to Barranco.

The eye surgery made me realize how much I was taking my eyes for granted. Mary Petillo, my aunt, went blind. Also my Aunt Sarah went blind. I was aware of those, and I thought that wouldn't catch me at all. I took my eyes for granted and, in a sense, I also took God for granted. It is really frightening when I take God for granted. I take my own life for granted. There is more that God expects of me than to take God or myself for granted. I learned that the eyes are a gift to me to do His work. I need to discover his work I am to do and not be satisfied with what I think is my work. Now I can understand why Jesus spent some time healing the blind, fulfilling what he had been anointed at his baptism to give sight to the blind. This is exactly what happened in my case. Through the people that were around me helping, Jesus helped me out with my sight.

Spiritual Director

It was Father Nicacio who heard about this project of the Diocese opening up a Seminary at the former Santa Familia Monastery. The Seminary was named after Saint Benedict. After my anniversary in 2013, I was a Spiritual Director of the new Saint Benedict Seminary in Santa Elena, Cayo, for five years. We haven't been encouraging our priests. We are lucky that we have four young men. This was a major change for me as I moved on from regular parish work to helping these candidates to become priests. We eventually had five Seminarians at the Seminary. Two dropped out and the other three continued. From the original group, we have Marcus Rodriguez, who is from Valley of Peace, was ordained as a Deacon in 2020 and as a priest in 2021. He was the first fruit of our labor at the Seminary. Then Mateo Salam, who is Qeqchi from San Pablo, Toledo, was ordained Deacon in 2021. I hope he will be ordained a priest in 2022. Shahir Pech, who is from Santa Clara Corozal, and Emanuel Medina, who is from August Pine Ridge, will be ordained Deacon in 2022.

Holy Redeemer

In 2018 Bishop Larry Nicacio invited me to return to Holy Redeemer to help out. I celebrated Mass four times a week, Sunday in Spanish, Monday, Wednesday, and Friday in English at the Chapel. Bishop Nicacio got a Spanish woman from Honduras, Nelly, to prepare my meals. I continued to see my doctors because of my prostrate situation every month, Dr. Aviada and Dr. Hidalgo. The beauty was that they didn't charge me for consultation, but I had to buy my own medication.

As a result of being a workaholic, I was burned out. There were different times that I experienced it, but it was really when my brother Sebastian took me to Dr. Cawich that the doctor made me face reality. Dr. Cawich said that if I wanted to live a few years, it was time for me to drop everything that I was doing, my pastoral ministry I should put an end to my work at Holy Redeemer and go home to my family to take care of me. When I reported this to Bishop Nicasio, he said, "You had better pack up your things and go home."

Retirement in Barranco

I had done my part and I needed to retire to Barranco. So I moved to Barranco where my brothers were working on my home. I got to Barranco in time to have my retirement home blessed by Bishop Nicacio.

Luke 5: 1 – 10:

1 Now it happened that he was standing one day by the Lake of Gennesaret with the crowd pressing round him listening to the word of God,

2 when he caught sight of two boats at the water's edge. The fishermen had got out of them and were washing their nets.

3 He got into one of the boats – it was Simon's --- and asked him to put out a little from the shore. Then he sat down and taught the crowds from the boat.

4 When he had finished speaking, he said to Simon, "Put out into deep water and pay out your nets for a catch."

5 Simon replied, "Master, we worked hard all night long and caught nothing, but if you say so, I will pay out the nets."

6 And when they had done this, they netted such a huge number of fish that their nets began to tear,

7 so they signaled to their companions in the other boat to come and help them; when these came, they filled both boats to sinking point.

8 When Simon Peter saw this, he fell at the knees of Jesus saying. "Leave me, Lord; I am a sinful man."

9 For he and all his companions were completely awestruck at the catch they had made;

10 so also were James and John, sons of Zebedee, who were Simon's partners. But Jesus said to Simon, "Do not be afraid; from now on it is people you will be catching."

San Lucas 5: 1-10 [in Garifuna. Accents are on the second syllable unless marked.]

1 Luagu ában dan, ñi ñein Jesusu láru dúna le gíribei Genesaret; ábati jayabingua saragu gürigia dari lun jámurdagúni, ladüga busen jamá jagaambuni lererun Búnigiu.

2 Ába larijin Jesusu bian ugunein málatu dúnarugu yarafa lun láru béya, rariguaaña esenijatiña tídaangiñe.

3 Ábati ládinum Jesusu tídoun ában tídaangiñe ugunein tuguya to luguneboun Simon, ába larengu lun ladisedun murusun lueí láru béya. Ábati lañurun Jesusu tídan ugunein, ába lagumerserun arufudaja joun güriga ñígiñe.

4 Dan le lásurunbei ladimurejan, ába lariñagun lun Simon. "Jeíba méme anagün, ábame jágurun ñi.

5 Lariñaga Simon lun, "Maesturu, ñadagimeinjadiwa sun áriebu mañaúguntiwa ni cáta; pero quei amürü lubei ariñagubalin, wágura."

6 Ába jágurun; dan le jiñuragunbárun séni, ñiñanu sarágu úduraü tídan darí yebe lun tajeiridagun.

7 Ábati jádügün seíñi joun jíbirigu ja tídaanbaba to aban ugunein lun jayabin ideraguaña. Ába jayabin, ába jabuinchagüdünun bíngubei ugunein darí yebe tadibiragun.

8 Dan le larijinbalin Simon Pedro cátei le, ába lájuduragun ligíbugiñe Jesusu, ába lariñagun lun, "Igira bána, Nabureme, ladüga ában wügüri gafigounti au.

9 Lariñagubálin Simon líra ladüga laweiridun lanigi, jáu sun ja úarabaña lúma, luaga añuguni le jadügübei.

10 Weiriti gine janigi Jacobo lúma Juan, ja lirajüñü Zebedéo, ja lúmabaña Simon. Ába lariñagun Jesusu lun Simon "Manúfudebá; lúmagiñe guetó buwadigimarida adíaja gürígia nun."

What Jesus said in Luke 5:10, that is what I have been doing, "catching people," what I am describing here as my life's journey.

Reverend Father Callistus Cayetano